Hidden In The Mind

A book of poetry

By Sara Scarlett

Illustrated By

Ethan Connery
& Emily Tonkin

Hidden In The Mind

Copyright 2018 Sara Scarlett

Printed in the United States of America

3-2-1 Press
An imprint of
Sunny Day Publishing, LLC

ISBN 978-0-9978006-0-9

Library of Congress Control Number: 2018930227

an imprint of
SUNNY DAY®
PUBLISHING, LLC

*Dedicated to all
of my family and friends
who have always
stood by my side.*

Table Of Contents

Welcome

You're going on a trip today. A journey of the human mind's deepest thoughts and desires. You'll go down many paths throughout your journey. You will visit the evils of the society that seems to control us. You will experience multiple feelings such as care, love, regret, and sadness.

Be prepared to open vaults with the strongest locks. Be prepared to walk down the darker tunnels that no one has ever walked through. You'll explore many different worlds, many different minds with many different feelings. Every poem tells a different story than the one before it.

These are feelings that all of us feel in our lives. It is normal to be emotional. It is normal to think deep into things. It is normal to be human. We were not made to be machines. Our organs replace our gears and parts. We are a living and breathing species.

We were made to feel, but what are these things that we feel? How do we explain our feelings? What are our deepest feelings? What do we really picture them as? Today, you will discover everything one feels in their life, maybe in a meaning much deeper than you can picture.

Dawn And Dusk

Glory rises over the horizon.
Bright colors represent the birth
of a new day.
Once dark is now light.
Once blind is now sight.
Eyes awake to a new world.
New stories are to be told.
For every day is something different,
Adventures embarked,
Experiences brought to life,
Until the night falls again,
When the world grows weary.
Peace is to be established
under a bright moon.
Whether golden or bleak, life goes on.

A Diamond Of A Woman

—Dedicated To Courtney

She is a rare gem.
Her heart shines brighter than that of the sun.
She takes the form of a beautiful maiden on the inside.
Those close to her never want to lose her.
They admire her personality within.
Those who despise her envy her.
They wish they had the heart she possesses.
She heeds no attention to those that want to be her.
And sticks by the ones who love her most
She is the original.
While the others are false versions of her.

Hearts Of Soldiers

Dedicated to all of the men and women who served our country

They fight day and night
For their country and for their families,
Willing to give their lives for freedom.
They are aware of the risks
But they set them aside
For they are the most courageous.
Their glory marches on.

Thank you for all that you do to make our country a
safer place!

Real Women

Her face may be unappealing.
Her body may not be entirely thin.
She may not wear a ounce of makeup.
Her eyes may be dull and show no reflection.
Some ask who would want to look into her eyes.
Her smile may not be the purest white.
Her hair may be a tangled wreck,.
Definitely not worth running fingers through.
No one dares to look into her heart
Where she holds true beauty.
She may not be physically attractive but she is loved
for who she is.
She is a goddess within.
Her heart is large, enclosed within it, kindness.
She cares deeply about those who love her.
She is polite and good mannered.
She is true, honest, and compassionate.
Those who use her are forever gone from her life.
She should be the one that men want.
Her looks do not stop many but her personality within
captures hearts
And that is how a woman should be loved.
Not for what she looks like but for who she is.

"Real women are hard to find. Once you run across
one, keep her. Treat her well and treat her true or else
she will leave and it will be very hard to find another
like her." —S.S.

Lonely

A stray dog sits on a cold
winter street.
His fur does not repel
the penetrating cold
that chills his skin.
He watches as the people
walk by ignoring him.
His eyes cry for help as
he watches them stroll past.
Across from him, a cat in the same
state as he, sits on a dumpster in an alley.
Except there are other cats nearby
But they prefer to stay away from her.
Something was missing in her life:
An owner who would love her
and not throw her out like her last
Which is how she ended up here.
The dog never had an owner.
And now that is all he ever wants
As both of them wait to feel complete.

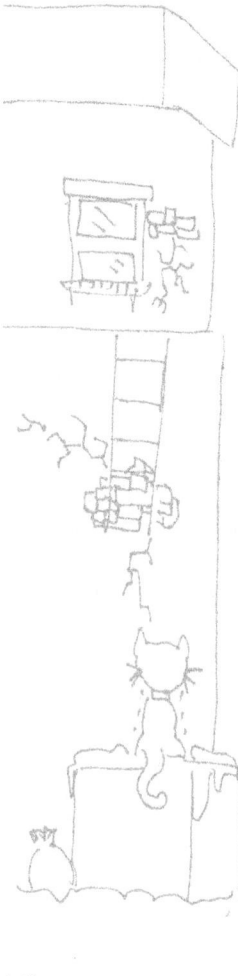

Fame

What would truly make a person happy?
Fame is a virtue we all would want.
Family and friends are also important to us
as humans.
There are two paths in life:
The path to fame and the path that the average
human takes.
Being famous has its perks but it would mean
becoming an icon,
Losing your human identity
And becoming a star.
The average path keeps you close to everyone in your
life that you love dearly.
And you value them more than anything.
Keeping them close to your heart and possibly
meeting new friends.
People all desire different things.
Pick the path you desire to hike upon.
And be careful not to fall off of the cliff.

The Abyss

Real monsters dwell in the depths
of society's dark waters,
Waiting for others to trust them and swim down their cliff.
They would think that the dropoff is a new path to
wanted freedom
But it only travels south.
After they become attached to the monster, it is too late.
As they are dragged into darkness.

Corruption Of The Mind

They are copies,
One made after another.
Everyone must be identical to be loved.
They try to take over genuine souls.
And transform them into copies of themselves.
There are some who do not wish to change,
who frustrate the copies.
They make the copies realize who they want to be like.
The copies try to be genuine but fail.
Once one is copied, there is no
returning to the genuine state.
They only advertise themselves as fakes.

Alone

I look like one of them
Yet I am not a mirror image.
I may be surrounded by them
But that does not make me one of them.
I do not act like they do.
I am different.
I am a rare species.
One whose members have long since gone extinct.
I sit alone in this wild jungle.
Desperately trying to find others like myself.

Haven

I wish I could take you away from your pain.
I do not wish to see you suffer.
I know it hurts.
I am hurting too.
Maybe we could run away together,
Away from all the cruelty of the world.
Come with me.
Take my hand,
Spread your wings,
And together, we will fly to a hidden paradise.

When Sadness Hits The Heart

Why did you have to leave?
Why did everything go wrong?
What did I do to lose you?
Now that you have exited my life,
A hole has formed within me.
One that cannot be patched.
I am missing my other half.
With a microscope to my heart,
Deep within I see
A gravestone with your name on it.
And I down on my knees
Weeping in front of it.
The air is gloomy and cold
As the rain falls from above.

Angel From Heaven

—Dedicated to Nash

He is an angel with wings that stretch out for miles.
His blue eyes sparkle in the sun's light resembling all
of the oceans and seas.
His smile glistens like snow resting gently on the
ground on a cold winter's day.
His heart is composed of the purest gold and his soul
twinkles with diamonds.
A halo made of these riches sits above his head.
He walks upon the clouds gracefully, never missing a
step.
Among all of the white ones, he spots a gray one.
He looks under the cloud to see a girl.
Her head looks down toward the ground.
Concerned about her, he flies down to see what has
happened to make her feel like this.
He does not even have to ask her.
As he notices her glass heart has shattered.
The pieces littered around her after a storm of disas-
ter.
He looks into her eyes.
She does not look up.
He understands as he feels the dark radiating from
her soul.
He finds all the shards of glass on the ground and
picks them up,
Connecting them together until her heart is recon-
structed.
It looks as beautiful as it once was.

17

She looks up at him, a lonely tear dripping down her
cheek.
He wipes it away and sits next to her, placing one of
his wings around her.
He told her that he'd always fly by her side and never
leave her to sit in darkness.
Darkness would lead to the pit of despair.
There would be no climbing out as the demons would
cover it with a large stone.
A smile appeared on her face.
She had forgotten the last time she had smiled.
She admired the feeling of happiness.
She had forgotten what happiness felt like until she
met him.
He embraced her with his wings,
Making her feel happy, safe, and loved.

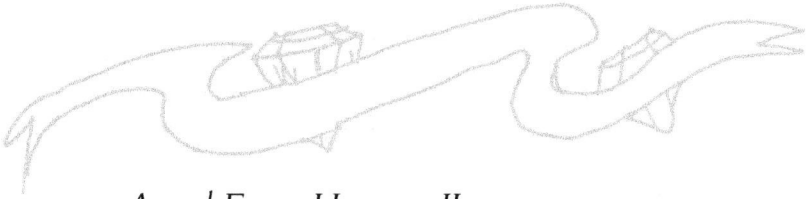

Angel From Heaven II
—Dedicated to Nash

I am the girl who lived this life.
The story that I tell is true.
I could always recall that day.
That beautiful day where an angel entered my life.
He was a gift from God
Sent down from the clouds above to be my comforter.
My angel,
My best friend,
My soulmate,
His words have stayed true.
He still flies by my side and never once has he left me
to sit in darkness.
The demons will not bury me as long as he is present
next to me.
His love is strong.
His embrace protects me from all of the evil.
It is my favorite place to be.
I am safe under his wings and in his arms.
He makes me a happier person as I try to find myself
after years of insecurity and self hatred.
I always pray that he does not fly away.
Because I love him more than everything.

Lucky

How was I blessed with you in my life?
How were the pieces put together?
The days that I have lived provided me with the
stepping stones to you.
We found each other
Both diamonds in the rough.
Maybe I heed not need to think.
No matter what road was taken from the day I was
born to this moment right now.
I am glad it was the road that led me to you.

Love Of My Present

My past has already been written.
I have already lived through all of the good times and
the bad.
I will never love those who dwell within the darkness
outside of my heart.
They can never re-enter the gates once they have left.
They betrayed me and treated me wrong.
My future has yet to come
But it looks bright ever since I met you.
You are an angel to my eyes
But your heart reaches deep into my soul.
As you and I may know, people change
And plans sometimes fail.
But I pray that I get to keep you.
I pray that everything will work out.
Throughout time we will face our trials.
We will have our fights.
We will have our conflicts.
I always pray that everything will turn out fine.
I will love you for now.
For you are the love of my present.
But Lord I pray that you will be the love of my future
And eventually the love of my life.

I Want To Show You What Love Is

You are lonely, yet undeserving of your state
You yearn for something hard to describe,
But I can describe it perfectly to you.
I want to show you what love is.
Frauds can send you into foreclosure,
But in my heart, I have built you an everlasting home.
The wrong arms can harm you and abuse you,
But in my arms, I have provided you eternal safety.
Sleeping next to me, you will never have to doubt,
worry, cry, or fear.
I will always ensure your happiness
I will provide you with comfort that no one can ever give.
You are my main priority.
You deserve the best in the world and I wish
to give it to you.
I will go out of my way for you just to see you smile.
Nothing harsh will ever be said to your face.
Because I cannot find one negative thing about you
after knowing you for so long.
You do not deserve the verbal cruelty anyways.
Your heart is too sweet and too kind.
You are everything I ever wanted and now I am
so lucky to have you.
You are one within billions.
I will care for you forever.
Then you will know what love is
My dear, true love is beautiful.

Mistakes Of Anger

I remember the time I crossed your path.
The way I looked at you I saw my soulmate.
You looked at me and saw your everlasting love.
Everything was promising for the two of us.
Then came the day where all of that changed.
I still wonder in my midnight thoughts.
Why did I erupt on you the way I did
When you did nothing wrong?
I had only gotten angry over something that meant
nothing at all.
That one mistake lead you to walk out of my life forever.
I guess I did not completely uncover your heart
As I bury it again.
Hoping someone else will find that buried treasure
That I was too greedy to have.

The Runner

He is determined.
A fire burns in his heart.
Everytime he steps on that track,
A new awakening,
A new goal,
A new adventure,
He never lets anything stop him
As he sprints towards the sunrise.

Champions

They are known to strive.
They are known to prevail over all the rest.
They are dominant and famed.
Some do not fit into the stereotype.
They are quietly the best at what they do.
They are humble with no need to boast.
Sometimes they are not famous.
Deep inside we are all winners.
Not all champions need to wield a trophy or wear a
medal around their neck.
They have silent pride in their hearts.

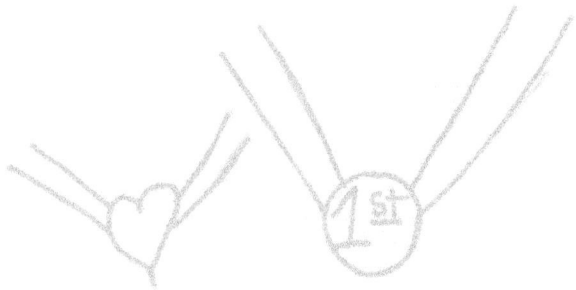

Trails

She walks alone.
Her white flowing dress brushes the ripples of the
water,
Her chestnut hair blowing in the wind.
Behind her she leaves her footprints,
Leaving behind all who have wronged her,
Leaving the times of regret and fearfulness,
Leaving her most depressing times as they evaporate
from her mind.
She fades into thin air leaving the lonely forest,
As her footprints become soaked in the riverbank and
vanish forever.
No one ever knew she was here.
She may have been a ghost in her old life
But she enters her new one an eternal spirit.

Snowflakes Of Thought

One by one they fall:
Family,
Friends,
Love,
Hate,
Friendships,
Dreams,
Goals,
Success,
Failure.
Why do all of these things fall
through the blizzard of our minds?
Because they are the attributes that make us human.

Abandoned

The sun cannot touch it.
In this realm, life cannot exist.
With the sky gray
And the grass brown,
Where wooden buildings decay, and fences fall apart.
History has chapters written here
But no one will ever uncover it.

Cloud Nine

All is fine.
All is well.
My life is perfect.
It feels like a dream.
I am flying.
Then suddenly my wings break.
I lose all control.
Gravity takes me away.
I'm falling.
I'm falling.
And there is no one below to catch me.

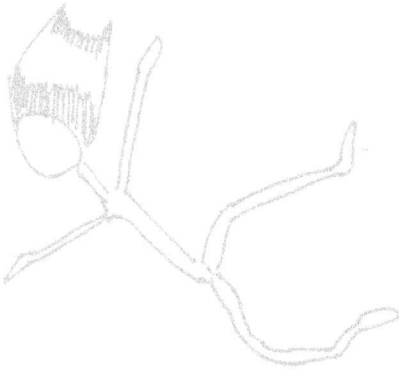

Facades

She is beautiful.
Her smile, white as snow.
Her hair flows in the wind.
She makes hearts melt.
Her eyes shine in the light
But behind those eyes lie evil,
Jealousy,
Hatred,
Sadism,
Antipathy,
She feels no feelings
Except the feeling of power.
Her heart has always been corrupted.
Only karma could bring her back to reality
And throw her into the deepest pit within Hell.

Mystery In The Stars

Gazing up into the sky tonight
I wonder to myself,
What could be out there?
My telescope can only see so far.
If only it could span the entire universe,
Maybe I would see
Someone from a distant world
Looking back at me.

Weather Patterns

Snow can fall and our hearts either be cozy or cold.
The sun can always shine and melt the ice,
Releasing the bright moments of our lives.
The rays reflect in our smile that others will see.
Sometimes, clouds can form in the horizon and bring
down rain.
Lightning may flash and thunder may crash,
But in the end, there is always a rainbow at the end of
the storm.

Beauty

Beauty beholds itself in every single one of us.
Although others may try to define it,
There is no true definition of beauty
As every person thinks differently and possesses their
own opinions.
We are all beautiful regardless of what we look like on
the outside.
Our true beauty is captured from within.

The Puzzle Of You

Your kindness,
Your respect,
Your honesty,
Your beautiful smile,
Your eyes,
Your true heart.
These are the things I love most about you.
Although I have loved you for years,
There is still pieces of your puzzle that I need to piece
together before I can truly understand you
And then we can grow together.

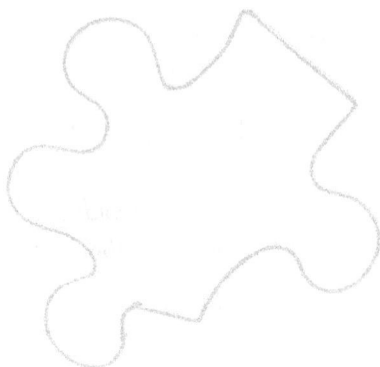

Shell Of A Man

He changed.
He was dissatisfied with himself.
Everyone loved him.
Now, all are confused by his actions.
He looks upon the people whom he
once called his friends.
They look happy but deep inside,
they are missing him.
He knows he should be with them
But he walks away.
As he becomes more distant,
his true self is banging his fists
on the interior of his eyes,
Crying for the force controlling him
to return where he belongs,
And to set his true self free.

Strength

Take your sharpest blade and strip me.
Of my skin,
Of my confidence.
Of my self esteem,
Or all of the above and even more.
Break me down until I become nothing.
I want you to watch me.
I will be suffering
But I will rebuild myself.
To be stronger than what I was before
And stronger than you.

The Judge And The Jury

Too young or too old,
Too thin or too fat,
Too ugly or too beautiful.
Too boring or too full of life.
The judge cannot tell me how to perceive myself.
The jury cannot tell me how to live.
There are no true standards.
We are all not the same nor perfect.
Only I have the final say.
I do not act like another.
I am not an identity thief.
I am myself.
That is the best anyone can be, themselves.
So why am I being accused?

States Of The Heart

A healthy heart is complete.
It does not need a lover to beat.
It is full of light and bright inside.
A broken heart may be damaged
But that does not mean it cannot be fixed.
It simply needs joy to be complete.
Finding happiness is a journey that many embark.
Sometimes, happiness is right around the corner.
It is just not always seen.

Magic

Oh what beauty.
Oh what serenity.
Run away with me into the night.
I will wear my glass slippers like Cinderella's at the ball.
If I lose one, I will have nothing to fear.
For I already have my Prince Charming.
Take me away in a pumpkin carriage.
Except, do not return me at midnight.
I do not wish to return.
I want to ride away with you forever
And live in a fairytale far from reality.

A Night Under The Stars

I like to lay on the soft grass with you.
Under the bright moon and the gleaming stars,
With the wind gently blowing through our hair.
I love the way your eyes twinkle in the moonlight.
I love how you caress me as we paint out all of the
distant constellations.
The stars map out our future.
Alas my dear, it is bright.

Rise

She is an angel.
Torn and battered.
The demons pull on her dress,
Attempting to drag her into the pits of fire.
Her wings have been burned,
Forbidding her to fly to the light.
The light is where she can finally be free.
Her halo may be dimmed.
Her wings may now be sticks.
She still has the strength to climb up the rocks,
The strength to escape her enemies once and for all.
So she can fly back up to exist within the heavens.

Hope

It does not rain forever.
A foreign species can thrive in a new landscape.
There is always another day.
Today might not have been yours
But you can be the ruler of tomorrow.

A True Man

He would run the farthest distance for her.
He would swim every ocean.
He would climb all of the hills and mountains.
He would give his life for her.
Only to make sure that she is safe, alive, and well.
His eyes are set on no other.
They will never rest on another.
He loves no one more than her.
Everything about her, he adores.
He does not want to find another.
No woman could match the traits of perfection and
beauty that she possesses.
Because they are not her.

Angel On Earth

She saves him without being near him.
She loves him without using her hands.
She heals all of his wounds without medication.
She takes him to a more beautiful place without driv-
ing him anywhere.
Words can go a long way from touching a heart to
saving a life.
If used right, they can give hope and meaning.
She tries to make him a better man everyday
And that is what she strives for.

Blind

Her mirror is a lie but through her eyes it is the truth.
She sees a face of her own that is full of flaws
But to others they see beauty.
She may think her smile is broken,
But someone in her world may think her smile is the
most beautiful.
She thinks no one could ever love her.
Little does she know that someone does love her just
the way she is.
She sinks deeper into the thoughts that she has told
herself.
She believes that all of them are true.
When those thoughts are lying to her heart,
making it shatter.

Valued

He feels worthless.
He compares himself with others.
He wishes he were stronger, better looking, and
smarter.
They beat him down to rubble.
He has what they do not.
He has a chivalrous heart.
He is not aware that he exists with fool's gold.
He is genuine gold that is just buried in the sediment
waiting to be uncovered.

Life

How beautiful it is to be blessed with life!
How fortunate it is to exist in a gorgeous world!
Be happy with what you have and ask for nothing more.
Let nothing take your happiness away from you.
It may get hard for you sometimes.
When you are bustling with work,
But always find time for yourself when it is all over and
enjoy the fun.
Darling, you deserve to be happy.
If you ever become troubled, come talk to me
And I will help you.
This world may be breathtaking but it has an ugly heart
when society is involved.
Live your life to the fullest and make it beautiful.
Never extinguish yourself of the journeys ahead
Or you will miss out on so much.
Remember your past, but do not live in it.
Enjoy the present
And anticipate the future.

Carousel

Around and around life goes,
Spinning in its eternal circle.
It halts briefly for new riders to select their horse
of choice.
One that they will ride down new paths on and
experience new adventures on.
Though after the passage of time, the carousel will
stop for some.
Some riders will get off and never return back on.
Even after they leave,
The carousel will continue spinning.

Escape

Banging on the dome of her skull
Is her inner self.
The thoughts dwell closer.
The stress rises.
She is about to erupt.
Everything happening in her life
comes together at once.
The pressure expands.
She reaches the point of no control
and she explodes,
Leaving her heart and mind to
suffer in her forest of dystopia.

Doll

It is what I have been my entire life.
Played with,
Tossed and thrown,
Dressed up to look pretty.
The patchwork designs of my face display a happy little girl.
Deep inside, I am destroyed.
Fluff pours out of my open stitches.
I may lose limbs.
I may lose parts of my face.
I may lose so much
But I can be sewn together again.

My Star

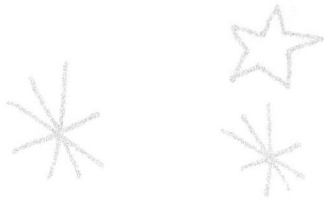

You are one in trillions.
You are the one shooting star that I wish upon.
You make all of my wishes come true.
When you fell down to earth, I caught you in my hands.
I climbed up a hill,
Gave you a kiss,
And tossed you back into the universe.
It made me cry a waterfall knowing that I had lost
something so beautiful.
But that is where you belong.
Years later, I stood on that same hill.
I thought of you.
I missed you.
I needed you.
What a mistake I made back then.
What a fool I was.
But you were happy.
Out of the corner of my eye, there was a twinkle.
I looked up to the sky to see a star falling.
The twinkle reminded me of the way you dazzled when I
first held you in my hands.
The star fell right next to me.
Its sparkle lit me up.
It was you yet again.
I held you and smiled.
I felt so fortunate to have you back.
I stood on that hill.
I gave you a kiss.
Instead of tossing you away, I walked home with you.
I put you in a jar.
So you could stay by my side forever.

Cleaning Regret

You did what you did.
There is no going back.
You chose that course.
You ended up hurting.
Others could be too.
Sure you can shower or bathe
Trying to wash the sin and pain away.
No matter how much soap you use,
You can never wash away the past.

The Pain Of Care

It is a pleasure to care.
It is a pleasure to use words and creativity to make
someone's day.
It brings happiness and smiles.
But do not allow yourself to be manipulated and used.
Do not allow yourself to be tossed around like a
simple toy.
Some do not know how to handle a real heart.
Do not follow too close to the wrong car
Or you might get brake checked.
You might not even apply your own brakes.
And it may cost you more than dollars.

The Final Day

If I knew it were my last day, I would spend it with you.
Knowing I would be gone by tomorrow,
I would want to hold your hand once more.
I would want to be wrapped in your final embrace.
I would want to feel your lips one last time.
I would want to feel your love
And nothing else.

Force

I told you to and you obliged.
I pushed you and pulled you.
You did everything that I said.
It felt good to be powerful.
Yet, I knew it was wrong.
I made you a toy,
Using you for my own benefit.
While, I provided you with nothing at all.
I am greatly sorry.
You were nothing but a pawn in my game.
And I wish you were a genuine jewel in my treasure
chest.

Mirror

Looking within, there is youth.
A young girl who is happy, bright, and full of life.
Time goes on.
Now in the same mirror, there stands a young woman
Putting on her makeup, awaiting her friends.
She returns a decade later.
She is not alone.
With her, a man and children.
Years pass.
The kids are growing and she is too.
She looks in the mirror one last time.
Only to see an elderly woman staring back at her.